Lost Souls

Poems From a Brown Girl

Dr. Sherron Gordon-Phan

India | USA | UK

Copyright © Dr. Sherron Gordon-Phan
All Rights Reserved.

This book has been self-published with all reasonable efforts taken to make the material error-free by the author. No part of this book shall be used, reproduced in any manner whatsoever without written permission from the author, except in the case of brief quotations embodied in critical articles and reviews.

The Author of this book is solely responsible and liable for its content including but not limited to the views, representations, descriptions, statements, information, opinions, and references ["Content"]. The Content of this book shall not constitute or be construed or deemed to reflect the opinion or expression of the Publisher or Editor. Neither the Publisher nor Editor endorse or approve the Content of this book or guarantee the reliability, accuracy, or completeness of the Content published herein and do not make any representations or warranties of any kind, express or implied, including but not limited to the implied warranties of merchantability, fitness for a particular purpose.

The Publisher and Editor shall not be liable whatsoever...

Made with ❤ on the BookLeaf Publishing Platform
www.bookleafpub.in
www.bookleafpub.com

Dedication

I want to dedicate this book of poems to those who have felt lost in this world. Those who have overcome trauma and yet continue to still feel alone. I hope and pray that one of these poems resonates as you continue this journey called life. May my poems make you feel seen, heard, and connected.
Remember, trouble don't last always...

Preface

This poetry book is called, *Lost Souls* because my soul has been lost between the reality of what is, and what the world wants me to be. I wander the Earth without a proper place to feel safe, to be loved, to be respected, and to be seen. So therefore, I called this book of poems, *Lost Souls* to help describe my feelings and journey into self-discovery and expression.
I hope this book helps someone and demonstrates that we are all human.

Acknowledgements

I first want to thank God, for giving me this opportunity to use my talents to help others. Thank you to my mom, dad, and baby sister who watch over me with their heavenly protection.

I want to acknowledge my son, Beaux' Phan. Thank you for being my inspiration to live, and to be the best version of myself. Thank you for always pushing me to pursue my dreams and reminding me that I am truly loved. Thank you to my friends who have stuck with me through this process and guided me out of some dark places. To my many students, thank you for allowing me to lead you on your writing and educational journey. I truly love what I do!

You always make me feel like the best professor on Earth!

Chocolate Mornings

I wake up with my Chocolate skin, Moca, Caramel, Cinnamon, Coffee.

Shades of me, shades of my ancestors, shades of supposed strength and beauty.

My Brown skin sparkles during the rise of the sun,
Making me feel connected, like I have already won.

But...nothing is perfect.
My life is not perfect.
My thoughts are not perfect.
My reactions are not perfect.
My plans are not perfect.
Nothing is.

I can see the lines, the cracks, marks, from the past.
I can see the trauma, the pain, the hurt.
I can feel the shame, as my body keeps score.

I struggle to find myself.
I struggle to stay grounded.
I struggle with faith.
I struggle to believe.

I struggle to stay alive.

Yet, I breathe, I live, I go forward, knowing my story, and knowing my purpose on Earth is not done.

The Beauty of it All

The air is sweet, salty, and wet.

The ocean sounds flow into my brain.

The blue watercolors bleed through my mind.

Washing away my pain, my memories, only momentarily.

The memories of trauma.

Despair, helplessness.

The soothing sound of water reminds me of safety, a womb like comfort that I miss, and I need.

The beautiful part is that the ocean symbolizes life's highs and lows.

Just like the tide, I shall return in due time.

Shine Shine Shine

The warmth on my skin feels like a kiss from the sun.

The brighter, the better.

The warmer, the nicer.

I need the Sun.

I crave it.

It gives me life.

Refill my energy, refill my hope.

Blind the darkness that has plagued me.

Shine light on the dark spaces no one gets to see but me.
Flush out the sorrow with light.
Making me feel like my future will be bright.

Shine, shine, shine.

The light can save me.

It can heal me.

It refills my hope.

So, shine, shine, shine.

Trapped Without a Key

You are trapped without a key.
You are trapped mentally.
You CAN escape what is not there.

What's trapping you?
Who is keeping you?
Y. O. U.
It's your mind, it's your thoughts, they're in YOUR control.

You are the key!
You are the answer!

Keys do lock, but...
Keys also unlock.

Remember, YOU control the key.
So, turn it.

So Eat

Turmoil, grief, pain.
Is this the recipe for a disaster?
Are these the ingredients to a useless? No!
These are the ingredients for a dish called LIFE.
Sometimes that dish is served up cold and spoiled.
Sometimes that dish is too hot to handle.
Sometimes that dish makes us sick.
Sometimes that dish kills.

To find out, we must eat it.
Swallow it.
And in some cases, devour it.
The more we eat, the more we learn what ingredients to add and what to remove.
The more turmoil, grief, and pain we experience, tells us WHAT to bring to the table.
It tells us WHO can sit at our table.
And WHEN to excuse ourselves form the table.
SO, EAT, RECOVER, LIVE!

More

I wanted more.

More laughter.
More cries.
More baby bottles.
More shoe ties.

I tried and tried.
I cried and cried.
Then tried and tried again.

I too died.

Maybe not the time.
Maybe not the place.
Maybe not the person.

Not knowing what life is for.

More...

Mirror

What is a mirror?
What does it reflect?

Does it reflect who we are?

Does it reflect what we are?

Does it reflect what we see?

Does it reflect what others see?

Does it reflect what someone said?

Does it reflect what's in our head?

Does it reflect the sadness?

Does it hide the madness?

Does it reflect the life we need?

Shatter those thoughts.
Shatter that chatter.
Break that mirror.

It's only glass.

I've Never Been Taught

Since the beginning of my life, I have been taught to honor God.
I have been taught to go to church.
I have been taught two plus two is four.
Water for a dry plant always needs more.

I have never been taught to care for Me, that I have feelings.
How to say NO with confidence.
How to honor MY wants before others.
You taught me some important basics.

Enough to survive, just enough to keep me alive.
Which sets me up later in life to eventually want to die.
Damn I wish I was taught.

You Didn't Make Me

My maker carries me across the sand.
My maker created who I am.
You did not make me.

My maker can separate unruly seas.
My maker prepared a future that I cannot see.
You did not make me.

My maker opens my eyes to see.
My maker calms my anxiety.
You did not make me.

You don't own me and never DID.
Your claim to me was INVALID.
You did not make me.

Age

Some say age is just a number.
I say, It's the date you enter life's journey.
Coming into the galaxy.
Dropping down and landing with those people who are your family.

Arriving in the form of a baby.

Sent to be taught how to nurture.
Sent to be taught survival.
Sent to be taught love.
Sent to be taught existence.

So, when people ask how old you just say...
Old enough to nurture.
Old enough to survive.
Old enough to love.
Old enough to exist.

Gather

People gather.
People have friends.
People have families.

Until it all ends.
What happened?
Where did they go?
I look around and still nobody knows.

Where is the life I knew?
The one I dreamed of.

I sleep.
Dream.
Nightmares.
I woke up.
Reality.
Life.

Remember when we ALL used to gather...

Jesus Hears Our Whispers

Jesus hears our whispers even if we don't speak.
Jesus hears our hearts, our hopes, and our dreams even when we're asleep.
Jesus hears our whispers and knows just what we want.
Jesus hears the doubt, the fear, the pain even when others taunt.
Jesus hears our whispers when we're crying in our sleep.
Jesus knows our darkest memories, the ones we don't want to keep.
Jesus hears our whispers when nobody seems to care.
When we are sad and lonely, know that Jesus is always there.

Comfort.
Love.
Peace.
Is in sweet Jesus's name.
Trust in him and the process.
You will never be the same.
In Jesus name.
Amen.

I Woke Up Sad Today

I woke up sad today.

Remembering why I felt this way.
Remembering the joy I had.
Remembering all the bad.
I woke up sad today.

Praying God washed those memories away.
But...
They are still here.
They won't leave.
They haunt me.
I still grieve.

I woke up sad today.
I guess some would say, hey at least I woke up.

Waiting

Stop waiting for that text.
Stop waiting for that call.
Stop waiting for someone to care.
Stop expecting it all.
Stop waiting for someone to give YOU life.
Stop worrying about it all.
Stop begging people to LOVE you.
STOP!
S-SLOW DOWN THOSE THOUGHTS!
T-TAKE CARE OF SELF!
O-OPEN YOUR MIND!
P-PERSIST YOU WILL MAKE IT!

Rain

Sometimes you need to walk in the rain.
To feel the wetness on your skin helps ease the pain.
Sometimes you need to get wet to wash away the fear.
To clean the surface of your body for others to get near.
Sometimes it's ok to walk in the rain.
The cold drops of water remind us of we're alive again.
Sometimes it's okay to walk in the rain.

For the rain can clean the stain and let you remain.
So, walk in the rain.
Play in it.
Dance in it.
Let it cover your whole body.
So go ahead and walk in the rain, live YOUR life, no need to explain to ANYBODY!

Searching...

Looking.
Wanting.
Searching...

I need an answer.
I need clarity.
I need peace.

I've been searching...
When are you going to call.
When are you going to speak.
That's right, you're busy.
You're too busy to talk.
Maybe tomorrow if there is time.
24 hours a day and not 10 minutes are mine.
Ahh, sex motivates you, now I see.

Still searching...

Cold

You have become so distant.
Pushed me away.
Silly boy, don't you know the heart wants what it wants.
It wants what it cannot have.
It craves the stolen moments.
The sweet kisses.
The warm hugs.
The long stares.
You have become cold.
Trying to freeze out memories.
Trying to freeze out future thoughts.
Trying to stop the dream of being with me.
Your heart has become so cold.

Yet I have become hotter than you can handle.
Warmer that the sun.
Your lips blister when they say my name!
Is that cold heart still trying to run?

Just go.
Remain the same.
Freeze me out.
Forget my name.
Forget my kindness.

Forget the joy we shared.
Forget that when you needed me, I was always there.

I'm too hot to handle!
Too bright to not shine!
I'm a supernova!
You have run out of time!

Feelings

We have a connection.
Hugs and kisses.
The kindness.
The way he smiles when looking at me.
Compliments.
The care I haven't had in so long.
It was familiar.
And I miss it terribly.
Panicking on what to do next.
What will happen next.
Not knowing what to say.
Scared and terrified of messing this up.
Shift shaping my personality.
Watering down my character.
Not being my true self.
Tired of losing in this love game.
I already lost, when I decided that I was not good enough.
He won a prize he did not earn.
While *I LOST MYSELF.*

Sometimes

Sometimes I need to be told I'm beautiful.
Sometimes I need to be told I'm missed.
Sometimes I need a bear hug and other times I just need a kiss.
Sometimes I need reassurance that you want me here.
Sometimes I need caressing and for you to pull me near.
Sometimes I need attention, and I need you to stare.
Sometimes I wish I had those things there.

Sometimes.
Sometimes.
Sometimes.

Who are we kidding?
It's All the time...

What Does God Do with People Like Me?

What does God do with people like me?
People who were hurt almost every day.
People who were young and didn't have a say.
How can we truly be whole?
How do we manage to pursue our life's goals?
How can we ever look at someone deeply in the eyes?
How can we do that while trying not to cry?
If you only knew what my poor eyes have seen.
If you only knew ALL my life people have been mean.
Kids should never fear the sun.
Kids should never have to fight, then run.
Kids are supposed to be protected.
Kids should never be neglected.

So, tell me God...
How does one give?
So, tell me God...
How long does one live?
With the pain, the hurt, the scars from life.
So, tell me, What *DOES* God do with people like me?

Sleepless Nights

You know...
The old folks used to say...
That if God wakes you up in the middle of the night, he wants you to pray.
He delivers an important message DIRECTLY to you.
He is trying to grab your attention because you have something to do.
God doesn't wake you up in the middle of the night for you to worry or to bring you strife.
He is trying to alert you so take heed.
He is trying to answer all that you need.
The old folks used to say God doesn't keep time.
Whenever he speaks to you there is no reason or rhyme.
Those sleepless nights are Gods way of keeping in touch.
He has plans for your future, let's just be clear.
All that you've been asking for is coming, my dear.
All that you cried for on those many sleepless nights.
He is guiding your footsteps child, *a little* to the left and 4 steps to the right.

The Wind Blows

The wind blows.
As cold as your heart.
As cold as Chicago in January.
It slams against my face.
It reminds me of the void of your warmth.

You used to be kind to me.
Sweet to me.
Caring for me.

Now, you are cold.
As I walk around.
Trying to forget you.
Trying to find myself again.
I can feel the wind blowing.
Kicking up the leaves and dirt like you kicked up my heart when I was settled.

You stirred up all kinds of debris.
Then you left and were gone.
Like the wind.

Infection

Bad thoughts are like an infection.

I can't.
I am weak.
I am not good enough.
I am not great.
I can't stop this addiction.
I can't be successful.
I won't find love.
I won't find peace.
I can't accomplish my goals.

What does an infection need to clear?

It needs medicine.
It needs rest.
It needs care.
It needs good food.
It needs good people.
It needs good thoughts.
It needs faith.
It needs peace of mind.
It needs YOU to say...

I can do it!
I am great!
I am worthy!

Until you are whole again.

Don't Poison My Joy

Don't come in and poison my joy.
Bleed in your sadness.
Covering me from head to toe in your misery.

Don't come in and poison my joy.
With your negative thoughts.
Your doom and gloomy outlook.

Don't come in and poison my joy.
It's crippling, it's deadly.
Your presence makes me ill.

Don't come in and poison my joy.
I want to break away from your darkness.
I wish you could take a pill.
To heal you.
To cure you.
To fix your narcissistic mind.
To help your outlook on life.
To actually be kind.

Don't come in and poison my joy because your life if filled with strife.
I'm better off not knowing you.

Before you my life was fine.

Don't come in and poison my joy.
Hang up boy and get off my line.

Tell Me

Tell me you miss me when I'm not there.
Telling me you miss me shows me you care.
Tell me what you miss and tell me how.
I want to know everything you're thinking, so tell me now.
How you miss my face or our cuddle time.
Tell me you missed me at a drop of a dime.
Don't hold back.
Tell me with all you have got.
Tell me you miss me or simply tell me not.

Part Of

I want to be a part of someone's heart.
Right there, somewhere between the left and the right ventricle.
I want to be a part of someone's heart and whenever they breathe, I gush through their veins along with their blood.
I want to be a part of someone's heart where they can't help but think about me every time it beats.
I want to be the warmth they feel when they're near me.
I want to be the reason their heart flutters when they touch my brown skin.
I want to be a part of someone's heart because it's their heart I truly want to win.

Tired

Tired of hearing sorry.
Tired of feeling lonely.
Tired of your mean words.
Tired of your excuses.
Tired of the lies.
Tired of tries.

Just tired...

Tired of your negative energy.
Tired of your dismissal of me.
Tired of always being on edge.
Tired of feeling as If I were dead.

Just tired...

Tired of the gaslighting.
Tired of feeling not enough.
Tired of letting you dull my shine.
Tired of YOU just making ME tow the line.

Just tired...

Tired of being of being sick and tired, I always jest.

Not exactly wishing for your *eternal* REST.
But...
Maybe then, I won't be so tired.

I Love Myself Today

I love myself today.
I love myself today.
I love myself today.

Although I messed up.
Although I made a mistake.
Although I failed that test.
Although I ignored my gut.

I love myself today.
I love myself today.
I love myself today.

Tomorrow I will try again.
Tomorrow, I get to start all over.
I am a good person.
I am human.

I love myself today.
I love myself today.
I love myself today.

Grace

Grace is not just something you say before dinner.
Grace is not just something you have when you curtsey.
Grace is the act of forgiving yourself for being human.
Grace is accepting your imperfections.
Grace is being kind to yourself whenever the world is cruel.
Grace is allowing yourself to heal however it may look.
Grace is taking one small step at a time.
Grace is loving yourself when nobody else does.
Grace is remembering you have overcome the seemingly impossible.
Grace is knowing to value yourself.
Grace is allowing yourself to cry.
Grace is allowing certain connections to die.
So please, please LEARN to give yourself the ultimate gift, of *grace*.

Fault is a Funny Word

Fault is a funny word.
It sometimes lays blame.
Especially from others who decided to play games.

Sometimes, fault is attached to a feeling or event.
Just know that all fault is definitely not heaven sent.

I blamed myself for years of pain.
It was so much pain that my eyes dripped like rain.
How can a child, a baby be at fault for an adult's pain?
How come that fault's pain still remains?

It does...
It wraps my body like a cloak.
Sometimes, fault's pain feels like being choked.
Fault is tricky, I do agree.
But this time, this fault has NOTHING to do with ME!

I See Glimpses of Beauty

I see glimpses of beauty while looking at me.
I see someone that I think is beautiful. Wow, very attractive!
Then, that feeling does not stick.
Then I'm reminded of my actual life.
I see all the pain in my eyes.
I see the despair.
I see the look on my face when nobody is there.
This beauty is so lonesome and so sad.
This beauty always ends up being treated so bad.
Why can't other see the beauty she can?
Then God reminds her that beauty is not defined by man.

Power

The power that was taken from me as a child was always meant to be given to those who lost their power.

It's just the transfer of power.
It's the energy shift that's needed.
It's the reason there was so much pain.
It was because I could handle it.
It was because I could be trusted with it.
I couldn't understand why, for so long and so many years I collected powerlessness.
I was collecting it and building up to then give it back to those who needed it.
To those who were robbed of their power.
To model what REAL power looks like.
So, they know how POWERFUL they are!

Understood...

Warm

Feeling the sun on my face feels warm.
Walking in the light.
Comforts me and I feel no harm.
Hearing the sounds of kids playing.
And the sports team's cheer.
Reminds me of all the things I've missed.
And wanting back those years.
Yes, I can't get them back, so I have to move forward.
Doing things that I do not want to do.
Accepting that I may always be a one and never a two.

Safe

So why is it selfish to want to feel safe.
To not walk around all the time with your head on a swivel.
To not constantly feel your heart racing every time you hear the patter of a certain someone's feet.

So, when is it self-centered to want to feel safe.
To want to breathe without hesitation.
To want to rest without fear.
To want to live without the date of an expiration.
To want to keep your loved ones near.

So why am I the strange one.
Why am I looked at weird?
Because I want to feel safe while I live out my years.
I felt safe in my mother's womb.
Some days, many days I wish I could go back.
Because who wants to be riddled with the constant fear of lack.

Honestly all I want you to do is to make me feel safe.
To get me back to that calming space.

Like

Like doesn't mean love.
Love doesn't mean like.
Often times people settle for like.
They are content with the word.
I don't mind the word like.
As long as it's not disguised as hate.
Most people use the word like to seem indifferent.
Most people use the word as a place holder.
Well, I don't LIKE that!
I don't LIKE being a place holder for someone else's love you pine for.
For a love that does not love you back.
For someone who doesn't respect you like I do.

Like can really hurt your ego.
Like can make you feel less than.
Like can make you feel not good enough.
Who wants to be liked?
Where can like take you?

Like is too safe.
Like is too easy.
I don't have to LIKE the word like.'
I don't have to LIKE it at all.

Why do we always say, "I like them but I'm not in love with them"?
Nobody should ever settle for the word like.
Like goes to bed early and never stays up late.
Like is second and love is first.
I need a word that I *LIKE and LIKE just* isn't it!

New Man or New Fan

Is this my new man or new fan?
Love bombing me with sweet nothings.
Saying... "good morning beautiful, hope you slept well".
Telling you via text how they miss your smile.
Late night talks.
Sexy talk sure sounds good after dark.
Filling my brain with dreams of companionship and promises.
Making me feel like I am the only one.
Talking talking talking.

Got me blushing without any proof of his promises.
When my brain and my gut is saying, boy bye...

Wanting wanting wanting.

Only time will tell...
Obsessive behavior.
Constant compliments.
I'm waiting for the shoe to drop.
I know, my brain has been telling me to stop.

That all depends on you baby girl.
You control what you want in your world.

Stop asking.
Start listening.
Walk away.

Surly time will reveal the answer someday.
Is this my new man or new fan?
Only God can say...

Slumming

Why does the world think that dating brown is a stepdown?
Dating black makes you have less tact.

Why do women who are a darker hue
must work way harder than some do to be noticed?

Why do we brown babes get the stares?
The side eyed looks from some and the compares.

Why are we dramatic, angry, too much of a hassle to date?
Why do some men look down on us expecting the worst and wanting the most?
Why do we brown babes always have to do extra to prove that we are worthy?

Why do we always have to be the strong ones?
Why are we riddled with the guilt and the weight of the world?
Where is it written that a woman that is black will always set you back?

Lies...

Sorry.
Love.
Understand.
My life is worthy.
My body is precious.
I'm beyond intelligent.
Now start treating me as so.
God makes no mistakes.

So Bad

Sometimes you want things so bad.
Things you hoped for, things you never had.

You pretend you do not feel the hurt and pain of life.
Never good enough.
Never ever been looked at it twice.

People steal your joy.
They take your spirit.

They kill your wants, your desires.
Hurting you because they are hurt.
Taking your light and dimming it.

I hate not feeling a part of this world.
It's not meant for me to live amongst the dreams of other nightmares.
Sorry just doesn't cut it anymore.

Waiting to Hear

We shared dream filled moments.
Waiting to hear.
We kissed, we caressed, we connected.
Waiting to hear.
We laughed; we talked all day and night for hours.
Waiting to hear.
Whenever we see each other, we hold hands for connection.
Waiting to hear.
I need your thoughts.
I need your heart.
I need your warmth.
I need you to speak freely,
Openly, lovingly.
Still waiting to hear.
Waiting, waiting, waiting.

Starting Over

Starting over is supposed to be painful.
Well not to me.

I look forward to the day where someone could match all my energy.
It's been so lonely in my head. I've started over many times.
Not knowing when, not knowing how, but believing it will happen in due time.
Accepting and creating a new environment may be hard to do.
As soon as I find someone that matches me, I'm swear going to leave you.
I deserve happiness just like anyone else.

You did this, you started it.
You bought this into our life.
You started this.
You did this when I became your wife.

It's time.
It's overdue.
I need to make a move.
I need to activate my faith.

I've suffered enough.
Time to take the first step.
Time to lay it all out on the table.

If I don't do it now, I may never be able.

Loneliness is Like a Hat

Loneliness is a hat we wear on occasion.
We wear that hat when people disappoint us.
We wear that hat when others abandon us.
We wear that hat when others fail us.

Loneliness is a hat we wear on occasion.
We wear when people hurt us.
We wear it when people lie to us.
We wear it when we hate ourselves.

Loneliness is a hat we wear on occasion.
We wear it when we don't feel enough.
We wear it when we are scared.
We wear it when nobody is around.

Actually, loneliness is a state of mind.
So, if it is like a hat.
Just take that hat off!

Who Do We Have?

Who Do We Have?
To save us.
To recommend us.
Who do we have?
To hold us.
To mold us.
To be okay with us being bold.
Who do we have?
When the world is cold.
When we are used for our talents.
Our bodies.
Our mind.
Who do we have?
When we need someone to be kind.
Who do we have?
When the world is against us.
When we're not longed for.
When we are misjudged.
Who do we have?
When we can't show anger.
When we can't be weak.
When we simply can't enjoy life.
Who do we have?
Who do we have?

Who do we have?
We have us!
We have each other!
Women we have us!
We're the only ones that know.
What it takes to continue!
What it takes to survive!
What it takes to be loved properly!
What it takes to be respected!
We are a rare breed of women!
And we need a special kind of person to see what we feel, live and need.
Who do we have?
We have the God that created us!
Actually, he's all we need!
He said he would give us the desires of our heart.
So, when you ask yourself who do we have...
We have EVERYTHING!

Painful Moments

Afraid to move.
The pain of you belittling me.
Constantly beating me down with your words emotionally.
Where is love?
Giving you a son was never good enough.
Where is love?
Finding ways to dim my bright light.
Where is love?
Making me feel helpless with no hope in sight.
Where is love?
The paralyzing trauma you brought into my life.
Where is love?
We took vows in front of God; I am your WIFE.
Where is love?
Not good enough.
At least you gave me a roof over my head.
Where is love?
Every night I try, then cry, wishing I was dead.
Where is love?
Got me questioning God's promises.
Where is love?
Looking for answers to why.
Why is this so painful?

Why am I hurting so much?
Your childhood was full of painful moments and times.
You Infused them in your mind and in your words.
Entering them into me.
Attaching the hurt from your life into mine.
That's NOT LOVE.

God, Please Forgive Me

God, please forgive me.
I'm not feeling like myself.
I've been waiting all my life to feel like somebody else.
God, please forgive me for these things that I want to do.
I've been so deprived, tortured all my life that I'm
looking for any glimmer of love, desire, want.
God, please forgive me.
I know I'm not perfect.
Give me grace.
Please.
Please.
Please.
Take this frown off my face.
God, please forgive me for my thoughts are so dark
currently.
All I want to know is why.
Why me, why?
Help me escape my tears and get them to run wet to dry.
God, please forgive me is all I seem to say.
I will keep repeating and chanting this mantra until...
I can fully walk away.

Move

Get up every day when your body tells you to move.
Didn't Madonna sing, "Get into the Groove"?
Your body was created with fantastic design.
Your body was built with specifically YOU in mind.
Your body serves a purpose.
Your body carries your frame.
Design for you to tackle life's stressful game.
Take care of it!
Treat it with care!
You only get one body.
For ONE DAY...it won't be there.
So... get up and move that well-oiled machine!
When we are cruel to our bodies.
They sure can be mean!

Lonely Day

It's a lonely day.
When you walk into *7-11* and the Decaf is out.
When you look around and no one is there to say, "good morning beautiful, have a great day".
When you wonder what today will bring.
Will it be today?
Will I encounter that person?
That feeling of fullness.
That tastes for satisfaction.
Driving through the city.
Watching folk's expressions.
Asking yourself, when will this loneliness end?

Lose Myself

I want to lose myself but see I can't.
I want to disconnect from this world, but I can't.
I want to lay down and cry, but I can't.
Sometimes I want to lay down and die but I can't.
I can't seem to disconnect.
I want to feel sorry for myself, but my spirit will not let.
I'm tired of trying to figure things out.
I just can't understand what the distance is about.
One minute you're close and then far the next.
You sure do have my peace disturbed and my heart vexed.
All I want to do is lose myself.
All I want to do is be someone else.
Lord knows I hate feeling this way.
Why won't God let me just lose myself today?

Been Fighting

I am always fighting.
Been fighting for years.
Fighting the sadness.
Fighting my fears.
Fighting the urge not to cry.
Fighting the urge not to give up and die.
Fight just to keep my good name.
Fighting just to stay in the game.
Sometimes I feel like I'm fighting for my life.
Even when the pain cuts deep like a sharp knife.
I always been fighting.
I guess it won't stop.
My inner voice tells me don't stop fighting girl, until your heart stops!

I Didn't See it Coming

I didn't see it coming.
All I saw was joy.
All I saw was admiration.
Someone who played coy.
I didn't see it coming.
The lies and betrayal.
I didn't see it coming.
So, fast our relationship failed.
What happened?
Why me?
Why did you target a pure heart?
Did you think you could manipulate someone who is smart?
Who we are kidding...
What does smart have to do with manipulation?
Anyone can fall prey.
The problem is that this smart woman decided to stay.
She didn't fight.
She played down her emotions and cried.
Many times, she even contemplated laying down to die.
So, why was I tricked.
My Rose-colored glasses kept your aura lit.
That's why I didn't see it coming.
He sought after me like a target.

But what exactly did he get.
He got something he will never ever have again.
Something that was beautiful.
So honestly, he didn't really win.
He delayed his OWN PEACE.
HE SPED UP HIS OWN KARMA.
NOW HE WON"T SEE WHAT"S COMING!
BECAUSE HE MADE HIS OWN BED!
Because he decided to mess with a chosen one, he gonna wish HE was DEAD!

Manifest

Manifest your life!

Say it!
Tell yourself its yours!

Say it!
Tell the universe you want more!

Say it!
Tell yourself what you want and say it with your chest!
Tell God what you want and make it your best request yet!

Say it!
Tell yourself loud and clear!

Say it!
So, the world can hear!

Do it!
Write it all down and make it plain!
Ask for your heart's desires in Jesus' name!

Do it!

Don't you dare stop!
Say what you want if you ever want to be on top!

I want this!
I want that!
I want him or her!

Say it again and again!

YOU manifest the life you deserve!

www.ingramcontent.com/pod-product-compliance
Lightning Source LLC
Chambersburg PA
CBHW060350050426
42449CB00011B/2912